Rise Up Women of God

Prayer Journal

Dr. Monique Rodgers

United States of America

Published by Shooting Stars Publishing House 2023

ISBN:9798399305837

Table of Contents

INTRODUCTION   7

DAY 1

Rise Up in More Love   9

Day 2

Rise in Strength   13

Day 3

Seeking Guidance and Wisdom   15

Day 4

 Finding Peace Amidst Chaos   17

Day 5

Nurturing Gratitude and Contentment   21

Day 6

Surrendering Worries and Anxieties   25

Day 7

Strengthening Faith and Trust   29

Day 8

Cultivating Forgiveness and Letting Go   33

Day 9

Honoring Self-Care and Restoration   37

Day 10

Embracing Divine Purpose and Abundance 41

Day 11

Rise and Shine forth for Jesus 45

Day 12

Arise with God's Favor 49

Day 13

You were born for this moment 53

Day 14

Rise up as finishers 57

Final Thoughts 60

About The Author 61

INTRODUCTION

In a world that often clamors for our attention, women are discovering the power and significance of rising up in their prayer lives. As they navigate the complexities of life, women are embracing the transformative practice of prayer, recognizing its ability to bring solace, guidance, and profound connection to the divine.

There is a rising tide of women who are realizing that prayer is not confined to mere religious rituals but is a gateway to personal growth, spiritual nourishment, and empowerment. In prayer, women find a sacred space where they can express their deepest desires, fears, and gratitude, knowing that they are heard by a loving and compassionate higher power.

The journey of rising up in prayer begins with a recognition of the unique spiritual essence that resides within each woman. It is an invitation to tap into the wellspring of divine wisdom, strength, and intuition that flows through their hearts and souls. As women embrace this truth, they step into their power and unleash the full potential of their prayer lives.

Rising up in prayer is a multifaceted endeavor. It involves cultivating a consistent practice, carving out intentional moments of stillness, and seeking authentic communion with the divine. It is about finding one's voice and speaking from the depths of the soul, knowing that prayers have the power to transform both the inner landscape and the world around them.

As women rise up in their prayer lives, they experience a deep sense of connection—to themselves, to others, and to a higher purpose. They find solace in moments of uncertainty, strength in times of adversity, and inspiration in the beauty of everyday life. They discover that prayer is a powerful tool for self-reflection, healing, and aligning their lives with divine guidance.

The journey of women rising up in their prayer lives is unique to each individual. It is a personal exploration that honors diverse beliefs, spiritual paths, and experiences. Whether through traditional prayers, meditation, journaling, or heartfelt conversations with the divine, women are finding their own authentic ways to connect and commune with the sacred.

In this empowering journey, women support and uplift one another. They create sacred circles of prayer, join together in spiritual communities, and share their experiences, wisdom, and insights. Women rising up in their prayer lives embrace sisterhood, recognizing the collective power of their prayers to create positive change and uplift the world.

As you embark on your own path of rising up in your prayer life, know that you are not alone. Countless women are on this journey alongside you, seeking to deepen their connection, ignite their inner light, and manifest their divine purpose. Embrace the transformative power of prayer, step into your authentic self, and let your prayers be the catalyst for personal growth, healing, and a flourishing spiritual life. The time has come for women to rise up in their prayer lives and illuminate the world with their radiant souls.

DAY 1

Rise Up in More Love

Scripture

*"Above all, love each other deeply, because love covers over a multitude of sins." -
1 Peter 4:8*

Love is the essence of our existence, a divine gift that permeates every aspect of our lives. It is the foundation upon which relationships are built, the force that binds us together as human beings. Love is not merely an emotion; it is a transformative power that has the potential to heal, inspire, and bring about profound change in our lives and in the world around us.

The Power of Love:

Love has the remarkable ability to break down barriers and dissolve differences. It is through love that we experience empathy, compassion, and understanding. When we approach others with a loving heart, we see beyond their flaws and shortcomings, recognizing the inherent worth and beauty in each person. Love has the power to mend broken relationships, reconcile differences, and create harmony in our interactions.

Love as a Guiding Light:

In a world often filled with chaos and confusion, love serves as a guiding light, illuminating the path before us. When we let love be our compass, it directs our thoughts, words, and actions towards kindness, forgiveness, and acceptance. Love empowers us to make choices that honor the well-being of others and promotes unity and harmony in our communities.

Love's Transformative Impact:

Love has the transformative power to change lives, starting with our own. When we embrace love as a guiding principle, it infuses our lives with joy, peace, and fulfillment. It softens our hearts, allowing us to experience deeper connections and meaningful relationships. Love inspires acts of selflessness and compels us to reach out to those in need, extending a helping hand and offering support.

Love's Healing Touch:

Love holds tremendous healing potential. It has the power to soothe wounds, both seen and unseen. Love provides solace to the broken-hearted, offering comfort and reassurance in times of grief and loss. When we extend love to ourselves, we embark on a journey of self-acceptance and inner healing, embracing our inherent worth and fostering a positive self-image.

Love in Action:

Love is not merely a sentiment; it is best expressed through tangible actions. It calls us to extend kindness, practice forgiveness, and lend a listening ear to those who are hurting. Love prompts us to serve others selflessly, seeking opportunities to make a positive difference in their lives. When we demonstrate love in action, we become vessels of divine love, bringing hope, healing, and transformation to the world.

Reflection and Prayer:

Take a moment to reflect on the role of love in your life. Consider the ways in which love has influenced your relationships, brought healing, and inspired positive change. In prayer, express gratitude for the gift of love and ask for guidance in cultivating a deeper understanding and experience of love in your daily life. Seek divine wisdom to embrace love as a transformative force, allowing it to guide your thoughts, actions, and interactions with others.

Love is an extraordinary force that has the power to shape our lives and impact the world around us. As we embrace the importance of love, may we strive to embody its essence in our thoughts, words, and deeds. Let us be vessels of love, radiating its transformative power and embracing the compassion, empathy, and unity it brings. May love be the guiding principle that leads us on a path of spiritual growth, fulfilling relationships, and a life that reflects the essence of divine love

Prayer:

Father God in the name of Jesus,

We come before you today with humble hearts, seeking your guidance and grace. We acknowledge that you are the source of all love, and we recognize our need for your wisdom and strength to love others more deeply and authentically. Today, we lift up the women in this world, asking for your divine intervention to ignite within us a fervent love that knows no bounds.

Help us, dear Lord, to love others as you have loved us. Open our hearts to see beyond the surface, to look past differences and shortcomings, and to embrace the inherent worth and beauty in every person we encounter. Grant us the ability to see through your eyes, to extend compassion, and to offer understanding even when it is challenging.

Teach us, O God, to extend kindness without expectation, to forgive without hesitation, and to lend a listening ear to those who are hurting. Fill us with empathy and the desire to genuinely connect with others, to hold their joys and sorrows as if they were our own. May our love be a balm that brings comfort, healing, and hope to those who are in need.

In our interactions, Lord, help us to be patient, gentle, and gracious. Empower us to speak words of encouragement and affirmation, to uplift and inspire others. Show us how to be selfless in our service, seeking opportunities to make a positive difference in the lives of those around us. Let our actions be a reflection of your love, O God.

We confess, dear Father, that at times we fall short in loving others as we should. We ask for your forgiveness for the moments when we have allowed pride, judgment, or indifference to overshadow our love. Fill us with your Spirit, that we may continually grow in love and become vessels of your divine love in this world.

As we embark on this journey to love others more, we surrender ourselves to your guidance, trusting that you will lead us in the path of love. Grant us the strength and courage to love even when it is difficult, and to persevere in love even in the face of adversity.

We offer this prayer, O God, knowing that you hear us and that you are faithful to answer. Thank you for the gift of love, and for your abounding grace that enables us to love others more fully. May our lives be a testament to the transformative power of your love.

In your holy and compassionate name, we pray. Amen.

Day 2

Rise in Strength

Scripture:

"I can do all this through him who gives me strength." - Philippians 4:13

As women, we often face challenges and obstacles that can leave us feeling weak and defeated. But as followers of Christ, we have access to a source of strength that is greater than anything we could ever muster on our own.

In Isaiah 40:31, we read, "But those who hope in the Lord will renew their strength. They will soar on wings like eagles; they will run and not grow weary, they will walk and not faint." This verse reminds us that when we place our hope and trust in God, He will renew our strength and give us the ability to rise above our circumstances.

So how do we tap into this strength? It starts with surrendering our weaknesses and struggles to God. In 2 Corinthians 12:9, Paul writes, "But he said to me, 'My grace is sufficient for you, for my power is made perfect in weakness.' Therefore I will boast all the more gladly about my weaknesses, so that Christ's power may rest on me." When we acknowledge our weaknesses and rely on God's grace, His power is made perfect in us.

Another way to rise in strength is through prayer and reading God's Word. In Psalm 119:28, the psalmist writes, "My soul is weary with sorrow; strengthen me according to your word." When we spend time in prayer and reading the Bible, we are reminded of God's promises and His faithfulness. This gives us the strength to face whatever challenges come our way.

Finally, we can rise in strength by surrounding ourselves with a community of believers who will encourage and support us. In Ecclesiastes 4:9-10, we read, "Two are better than one, because they have a good return for their labor: If either of them falls down, one can help the other up. But pity anyone who falls and has no one to help them up." When we have a community of believers who will lift us up and pray for us, we are strengthened and encouraged to keep going.

So today, let us rise in strength by surrendering our weaknesses to God, spending time in prayer and reading His Word, and surrounding ourselves with a community of believers. With God's help, we can soar on wings like eagles and face whatever challenges come our way with confidence and strength.

Prayer:

Dear Heavenly Father,

We come before you today as women who are in need of your strength. We face challenges and obstacles that can leave us feeling weak and defeated, but we know that with you, all things are possible.

We ask that you renew our strength and give us the ability to rise above our circumstances. Help us to surrender our weaknesses and struggles to you, knowing that your grace is sufficient for us. May your power be made perfect in our weakness.

We pray that you would give us a hunger for your Word and a desire to spend time in prayer. Remind us of your promises and your faithfulness, and give us the strength to face whatever challenges come our way.

We also ask that you surround us with a community of believers who will encourage and support us. Help us to be vulnerable with one another and to lift each other up in prayer.

Thank you for the strength that you provide, and for the ways in which you have already carried us through difficult times. We trust in your goodness and your faithfulness, and we know that with you, we can rise in strength. In Jesus' name we pray, Amen.

Day 3

Seeking Guidance and Wisdom

Scripture:

"Trust in the LORD with all your heart and lean not on your own understanding; in all your ways submit to him, and he will make your paths straight." - Proverbs 3:5-6

As women, we are constantly seeking to grow and improve ourselves. One of the most valuable things we can seek is wisdom. Proverbs 4:7 tells us, "The beginning of wisdom is this: Get wisdom. Though it costs all you have, get understanding." This verse reminds us that wisdom is worth pursuing, even if it requires sacrifice.

So how do we seek wisdom? It starts with recognizing that true wisdom comes from God. In James 1:5, we read, "If any of you lacks wisdom, you should ask God, who gives generously to all without finding fault, and it will be given to you." When we ask God for wisdom, He promises to give it to us generously.

Another way to seek wisdom is through reading and studying God's Word. In Psalm 119:105, the psalmist writes, "Your word is a lamp for my feet, a light on my path." When we spend time in the Bible, we are reminded of God's wisdom and His ways. This helps us to make wise decisions and to live in a way that honors Him.

We can also seek wisdom by seeking out wise counsel from others. Proverbs 15:22 says, "Plans fail for lack of counsel, but with many advisers they succeed." When we seek advice from those who are wise and experienced, we can gain valuable insights and avoid making costly mistakes.

Finally, we can seek wisdom by being open to learning and growing. Proverbs 9:9 tells us, "Instruct the wise and they will be wiser still; teach the righteous and they will add to their learning." When we are willing to learn from others and to admit our own shortcomings, we can grow in wisdom and become better equipped to face the challenges of life.

So today, let us seek more wisdom by asking God for it, spending time in His Word, seeking wise counsel from others, and being open to learning and growing. May we be women who are known for our wisdom and discernment, and may we use that wisdom to bring glory to God and to bless those around us.

Prayer:

Dear Heavenly Father,

We come before you today as women who desire to grow in wisdom. We recognize that true wisdom comes from you, and we ask that you would give us the wisdom we need to navigate the challenges of life.

We ask that you would give us a hunger for your Word and a desire to spend time in prayer. May your Word be a lamp for our feet and a light on our path, guiding us in the way we should go.

We also ask that you would surround us with wise counsel. Help us to seek out those who are experienced and knowledgeable, and give us the discernment to know when to listen and when to speak.

We pray that you would help us to be open to learning and growing. Give us the humility to admit our own shortcomings and the willingness to learn from others.

Above all, we ask that you would help us to use the wisdom you give us to bring glory to you and to bless those around us. May we be women who are known for our wisdom and discernment, and may we use that wisdom to make a positive impact in the world.

Thank you for your faithfulness and your goodness. We trust in your wisdom and your guidance, and we know that with you, all things are possible. In Jesus' name we pray, Amen.

Day 4

Finding Peace Amidst Chaos

Scripture:

"Peace I leave with you; my peace I give you. I do not give to you as the world gives. Do not let your hearts be troubled and do not be afraid." - John 14:27

As women, we often find ourselves juggling multiple responsibilities and facing a never-ending to-do list. It can be easy to feel overwhelmed and stressed out, especially when unexpected challenges arise. But as followers of Christ, we have access to a peace that surpasses all understanding.

In John 14:27, Jesus says, "Peace I leave with you; my peace I give you. I do not give to you as the world gives. Do not let your hearts be troubled and do not be afraid." This verse reminds us that the peace that Jesus gives us is not like the peace that the world offers. It is a deep and abiding peace that can sustain us even in the midst of chaos.

So how do we find this peace? It starts with surrendering our worries and fears to God. In Philippians 4:6-7, we read, "Do not be anxious about anything, but in every situation, by prayer and petition, with thanksgiving, present your requests to God. And the peace of God, which transcends all understanding, will guard your hearts and your minds in Christ Jesus." When we bring our concerns to God in prayer, He promises to give us a peace that transcends all understanding.

Another way to find peace in the midst of chaos is by focusing on God's promises. In Isaiah 26:3, we read, "You will keep in perfect peace those whose minds are steadfast, because they trust in you." When we trust in God's promises and keep our minds fixed on Him, we can experience a peace that is not dependent on our circumstances.

We can also find peace by taking care of ourselves physically, emotionally, and spiritually. This means getting enough rest, eating well, exercising, and spending time in prayer and meditation. When we take care of ourselves, we are better equipped to handle the challenges that come our way.

Finally, we can find peace by leaning on our community of believers. In Galatians 6:2, we read, "Carry each other's burdens, and in this way you will fulfill the law of Christ." When we share our struggles with others and allow them to support us, we can experience a sense of peace and comfort that comes from knowing we are not alone.

So today, let us find peace in the midst of chaos by surrendering our worries to God, focusing on His promises, taking care of ourselves, and leaning on our community of believers. May we be women who are known for our peace and calm in the face of adversity, and may we use that peace to bring glory to God and to bless those around us.

Prayer:

Dear Heavenly Father,

We come before you today as women who are facing chaos and uncertainty. We feel overwhelmed and stressed out, and we need your peace to sustain us.

We ask that you would help us to surrender our worries and fears to you. May we bring our concerns to you in prayer, knowing that you promise to give us a peace that transcends all understanding.

We also ask that you would help us to focus on your promises. May we keep our minds fixed on you, trusting in your goodness and your faithfulness even in the midst of chaos.

We pray that you would help us to take care of ourselves physically, emotionally, and spiritually. Give us the strength to get enough rest, to eat well, to exercise, and to spend time in prayer and meditation.

Finally, we ask that you surround us with a community of believers who will support and encourage us. May we be willing to share our struggles with others and to allow them to carry our burdens with us.

Thank you for your peace that surpasses all understanding. We trust in your goodness and your faithfulness, and we know that with you, all things are possible. In Jesus' name we pray, Amen.

Day 5

Nurturing Gratitude and Contentment

Scripture:

"Give thanks in all circumstances; for this is God's will for you in Christ Jesus."
- 1 Thessalonians 5:18

As women, we often find ourselves striving for more. We want more success, more money, more recognition, and more possessions. But the pursuit of more can leave us feeling empty and unfulfilled. The antidote to this discontentment is gratitude and contentment.

In 1 Thessalonians 5:18, we read, "Give thanks in all circumstances; for this is God's will for you in Christ Jesus." This verse reminds us that gratitude is not dependent on our circumstances. We can choose to be thankful even in the midst of difficult situations.

So how do we cultivate gratitude and contentment? It starts with recognizing the blessings that we already have. When we take the time to count our blessings and to give thanks for them, we are reminded of God's goodness and faithfulness.

Another way to cultivate gratitude and contentment is by focusing on the present moment. When we are constantly looking ahead to the next thing, we miss out on the beauty and joy that is right in front of us. By being present in the moment and savoring the blessings that we have right now, we can experience a sense of contentment and peace.

We can also cultivate gratitude and contentment by serving others. When we focus on the needs of others and seek to bless them, we are reminded of how much we have to be thankful for. Serving others also helps us to put our own problems and concerns into perspective.

Finally, we can cultivate gratitude and contentment by trusting in God's provision. In Philippians 4:19, we read, "And my God will meet all your needs according to the riches of his glory in Christ Jesus." When we trust in God's provision and His timing, we can experience a sense of peace and contentment that comes from knowing that He is in control.

So today, let us cultivate gratitude and contentment by counting our blessings, being present in the moment, serving others, and trusting in God's provision. May we be women who are known for our gratitude and contentment, and may we use that gratitude to bring glory to God and to bless those around us.

Prayer:

Father God in the name of Jesus,

We come before you today with humble hearts, seeking your guidance and blessings. We lift up women everywhere and ask for your divine intervention in granting them the gift of contentment. In a world that often breeds comparison, self-doubt, and unattainable standards, we ask for your comforting presence to bring peace and satisfaction to the hearts of women.

Lord, instill within us a deep sense of self-worth, reminding us that we are fearfully and wonderfully made. Help us embrace our unique qualities, strengths, and weaknesses, knowing that each aspect of our being contributes to the tapestry of your creation. Teach us to find contentment in who we are, for we are truly enough just as we are.

In moments of dissatisfaction and restlessness, Lord, grant us the wisdom to recognize the blessings that surround us. Open our eyes to the beauty of life's simple pleasures—the warmth of sunlight, the fragrance of blooming flowers, the laughter of loved ones. Help us find joy in the present moment, rather than constantly longing for what lies beyond our grasp.

Guide us to cherish and nurture the relationships we hold dear. Grant us the ability to love and be loved, to find solace and support in the companionship of family and friends. May our interactions with others be filled with kindness, empathy, and understanding, fostering an environment of mutual respect and appreciation.

Help us to cultivate gratitude in our hearts, for gratitude breeds contentment. Let us acknowledge and give thanks for the blessings we have been bestowed, both big and small. Open our eyes to the countless miracles that unfold in our lives each day, reminding us of your everlasting love and care.

Lord, we surrender our fears and worries to you, knowing that you are our ultimate source of peace. Help us release the burdens of comparison, perfectionism, and societal expectations. Grant us the strength to embrace our individual journeys, trusting that you have a purpose for each one of us.

May we find contentment not solely in material possessions or achievements but in a deeper connection with you, dear Lord. Nurture our spirits, aligning our desires with your will. Teach us to seek fulfillment in serving others, in acts of compassion and selflessness.

Finally, Lord, grant us the courage to walk confidently in our purpose, embracing the unique path you have set before us. Strengthen our faith, reminding us that your plans for us are good and that you are always with us, guiding us every step of the way.

We offer this prayer, trusting in your infinite wisdom and love. May you fill the hearts of all women with contentment, empowering them to live lives that honor and glorify you.

In your holy and precious name, we pray. Amen.

Day 6

Surrendering Worries and Anxieties

Scripture:

"Do not be anxious about anything, but in every situation, by prayer and petition, with thanksgiving, present your requests to God. And the peace of God, which transcends all understanding, will guard your hearts and your minds in Christ Jesus." - Philippians 4:6-7

Scripture:

"Therefore I tell you, do not worry about your life, what you will eat or drink; or about your body, what you will wear. Is not life more than food, and the body more than clothes?" - Matthew 6:25 (NIV)

Dear Sisters,

In the busyness of our lives, worry can easily consume our thoughts and drain our spirits. The weight of responsibilities, uncertainties, and expectations can leave us feeling overwhelmed and anxious. But today, let us draw strength from God's Word as we embark on a journey towards releasing worry and embracing a life filled with peace.

Our heavenly Father, who knows us intimately, invites us to cast our worries upon Him. He understands the burdens we carry, and He longs to exchange them for His peace. In Matthew 6:25, Jesus lovingly reminds us not to worry about the things that consume our minds— our daily needs, our appearance, or the uncertainties of the future. He reminds us that life is about so much more.

Sisters, worry hinders us from fully experiencing the abundant life that Christ offers. It robs us of our joy and contentment, and it distracts us from the present moment. Worry causes us to focus on what we lack rather than on the goodness of our God, who is our provider and sustainer.

So, how can we release worry and embrace a life of peace? It begins with surrender. Surrendering our worries to God is an act of faith, acknowledging that He is in control and that His plans for us are good. As we surrender, we can trust that God's love for us is unwavering, and His faithfulness will guide us through every circumstance.

Sisters, let us also remember that worry is not a burden we were meant to carry alone. We have a loving Savior who invites us to bring our worries to Him in prayer. Through prayer, we can pour out our concerns, fears, and anxieties before God, knowing that He hears us. In Philippians 4:6, we are encouraged to present our requests to God with thanksgiving. As we do so, His peace, which surpasses all understanding, will guard our hearts and minds.

Furthermore, let us surround ourselves with a community of believers who can offer support, encouragement, and prayer. As we share our burdens with trusted sisters in Christ, we allow God's love to flow through their words and actions, comforting and strengthening us.

Lastly, sisters, let us fix our minds on the truth of God's Word. Meditate on His promises and remember His faithfulness throughout history. Recall the times when He provided, protected, and guided His people. As we fill our minds with the truth, the lies of worry lose their power, and we can rest assured that God is with us in every situation.

Today, let us release the burden of worry and embrace the peace that surpasses all understanding. Remember, dear sisters, that worry cannot add a single moment to our lives, but it can steal the joy from each moment we have been given. Trust in God's faithfulness, surrender your worries to Him, and allow His peace to guide your steps.

Prayer:

Heavenly Father,

Today, we come before You, weary from the weight of worry. We lay our burdens at Your feet, trusting that You are our loving and faithful provider. Help us, Lord, to release the grip of worry on our lives and to embrace Your peace that surpasses all understanding.

In moments of anxiety, remind us of Your presence. May Your Spirit guide us, filling our minds with Your truth and comforting our hearts with Your love

Loving Father,

We humbly come before You, acknowledging that worry has crept into our lives and burdened our hearts. Today, we lift up the women who are carrying the weight of anxiety, fear, and uncertainty. We ask for Your divine intervention and the touch of Your healing hand upon their lives.

Lord, You know the intricacies of each woman's journey—the challenges they face, the responsibilities they bear, and the dreams they hold dear. Yet, You remind us in Your Word not to worry but to trust in Your provision and faithfulness. Help us to surrender our worries to You, for You are the source of all wisdom, strength, and peace.

In moments of doubt, remind us of Your steadfast love. Your love is a refuge and a shelter, shielding us from the storms of life. Teach us to cast our anxieties upon You, knowing that You care deeply for us and have a perfect plan for our lives. Help us to trust in Your timing and Your ways, even when the path before us seems uncertain.

Father, we confess that worry can consume our thoughts and drain our spirits. But today, we choose to fix our eyes on You—the author and perfecter of our faith. Renew our minds and transform our perspective. Help us to focus on the things that are true, noble, just, pure, lovely, and praiseworthy, as Your Word instructs.

In moments of fear, remind us of Your power. You are the Almighty God who calms the raging storms, who brings order out of chaos, and who gives strength to the weary. Fill us with Your peace that transcends all understanding, guarding our hearts and minds in Christ Jesus.

Lord, we ask for a spirit of discernment to recognize the difference between productive concern and paralyzing worry. Give us the courage to surrender our need for control and to trust in Your sovereignty. Help us to surrender our plans and desires to Your perfect will, knowing that Your ways are higher than our own.

We pray for unity and support among women, that we may lift each other up in prayer and encouragement. Surround us with wise and loving sisters who will remind us of Your promises and spur us on in faith. May our relationships be marked by authenticity, vulnerability, and grace, as we navigate life's challenges together.

Father, we lay before You our worries about the future, our concerns about our families, our careers, our health, and our relationships. We release them into Your capable hands, knowing that You are able to work all things together for our good.

Finally, Lord, help us to live in the present moment, cherishing the blessings You have bestowed upon us. Open our eyes to the beauty that surrounds us—the gentle touch of a breeze, the warmth of the sun, the laughter of loved ones. Help us to cultivate an attitude of gratitude, finding joy in the small miracles that unfold in our lives each day. In Your loving and compassionate name, we pray. Amen.

Day 7

Strengthening Faith and Trust

Scripture:

"For we live by faith, not by sight." - 2 Corinthians 5:7

"She is clothed with strength and dignity; she can laugh at the days to come." - Proverbs 31:25 (NIV)

Devotional:

Dear Sisters,

In a world filled with uncertainty, challenges, and unexpected twists, we often find ourselves yearning for strength, faith, and trust. As women, we face unique struggles, and at times, we may feel overwhelmed or inadequate. But today, let us turn our gaze toward the One who equips us and empowers us to rise above every circumstance.

In Proverbs 31, we read about a woman who exemplifies strength and dignity. She embodies the qualities we aspire to possess—resilience, wisdom, and an unwavering trust in God's plan. Like her, we are called to clothe ourselves with strength, not in our own might, but in the strength that comes from our Heavenly Father.

True strength, dear sisters, is not measured by physical might or independence, but by our willingness to surrender to God's leading and to rely on His power in every situation. It is found in our vulnerability before Him, recognizing that it is in our weakness that His strength is made perfect (2 Corinthians 12:9).

As women of faith, our strength is rooted in our relationship with

God. It is through our connection with Him that we draw the courage to face challenges head-on, knowing that He is our refuge and fortress (Psalm 91:2). In times of hardship, we can find solace in His promises, trusting that He will never leave us nor forsake us (Hebrews 13:5).

Faith, dear sisters, is the anchor that holds us firm when the storms of life threaten to shake us. It is a steadfast belief in the goodness, faithfulness, and sovereignty of our Heavenly Father. Like the woman described in Proverbs 31, we can face the future with a confident hope, knowing that God holds every moment in His hands.

When doubts and fears arise, let us turn to the pages of Scripture. In God's Word, we find countless stories of women who displayed unwavering faith and trust in the face of adversity. From Esther's courage to stand for her people, to Mary's surrender to God's plan, their examples remind us that we too can find strength and faith in our Creator.

Trusting in God requires us to relinquish our own understanding and to lean on His wisdom. It may not always be easy or comfortable, but as we surrender our plans and desires to Him, we allow Him to guide our steps and bring about His perfect will. Our trust in Him is a declaration that we believe His ways are higher than our own (Isaiah 55:9).

Sisters, let us remember that our strength, faith, and trust are not based on our own capabilities but on the unchanging character of our Heavenly Father. He is the same yesterday, today, and forever (Hebrews 13:8). In Him, we find an unshakeable foundation, a rock on which we can build our lives.

Today, let us embrace the strength, faith, and trust that God offers us. Clothed in His power, let us face each day with confidence, knowing that He goes before us, walks beside us, and carries us through every season. May we be women who stand strong, who live by faith, and who trust in the unfailing love of our Heavenly Father.

Prayer:

Gracious Father,

We come before You in awe of Your strength, faithfulness, and love. Thank You for equipping us with the strength we need to navigate the challenges of life. Help us to trust in Your wisdom and to rely on Your power in every circumstance.

When we feel weak or inadequate, remind us of Your unwavering strength that resides within us. Teach us to surrender our fears, doubts, and worries to You, knowing that You are our refuge and fortress. Fill us with the confidence that comes from knowing You are always with us.

Strengthen our faith, dear Lord, that we may believe in Your goodness and faithfulness even when circumstances seem bleak. Open our hearts to receive Your promises and let them anchor our souls in times of uncertainty. Help us to rely on Your Word, which is a lamp to our feet and a light to our path.

Lord, in our moments of doubt, remind us of the women of faith who have gone before us. Their stories inspire us to trust You fully and to embrace Your plan for our lives. May we draw strength from their examples and find encouragement in the testimonies of Your faithfulness throughout history.

We surrender our plans and desires to You, dear Father, trusting that Your ways are higher than our own. Guide our steps, and help us to align our will with Yours. Give us the patience and wisdom to wait on Your perfect timing, knowing that You work all things together for our good.

Thank You, Lord, for the unshakable strength, faith, and trust that we find in You. May we live each day as women who are clothed in Your power and who reflect Your love to the world.

In Jesus' name, we pray.

Amen.

In this sacred moment, we humbly come before you, seeking your grace and guidance. Today, we lift up our voices in prayer, asking for your blessings upon the women of the world. Surround them with your love, light, and boundless strength. Grant them unwavering faith and the resilience to face life's challenges with courage and grace.

We pray for the women who are striving to create a better future for themselves and their loved ones. Inspire them with wisdom and clarity, that they may pursue their dreams and aspirations with unwavering determination. Help them to recognize their inherent worth and capabilities, empowering them to unleash their potential to the fullest.

Grant strength to the women who are struggling in the face of adversity. Provide them with solace in times of hardship, reminding them that they are never alone. Shower them with compassion and resilience, so they may find the inner strength to rise above any obstacles they encounter.

May the women who are burdened with responsibilities find the support they need. Grant them the energy and endurance to fulfill their numerous roles with grace and love. Help them find balance in their lives, knowing when to rest and restore their spirits.

Guide the women who are seeking their true purpose in life. Illuminate their paths, revealing their unique gifts and talents. Fill their hearts with passion and conviction, enabling them to make a positive impact on the world around them. Encourage them to embrace their authentic selves, breaking free from societal limitations and expectations.

Father, instill unwavering faith in the hearts of all women. Strengthen their connection to their inner divine essence. Remind them of their infinite worth, their inherent beauty, and the profound impact they have on the lives they touch.

May they find solace in times of doubt, knowing that you are always by their side, guiding their steps and supporting their journey. Grant them the wisdom to recognize the miracles that unfold within their lives each day, nurturing their faith and inspiring them to embrace the fullness of their existence.

In your divine presence, we place our prayers for the women of the world. May they be blessed with abundant strength, unshakable faith, and unwavering love. Amen.

Day 8

Cultivating Forgiveness and Letting Go

Scripture:

"Bear with each other and forgive one another if any of you has a grievance against someone. Forgive as the Lord forgave you." - Colossians 3:13

Scripture:

"Bear with each other and forgive one another if any of you has a grievance against someone. Forgive as the Lord forgave you." - Colossians 3:13 (NIV)

Devotional:

Dear Sisters,

Forgiveness is a powerful act that holds the key to our emotional healing and spiritual growth. As women who have experienced hurt, betrayal, or disappointment, we understand the weight that unforgiveness can place upon our hearts. But today, let us embark on a journey of forgiveness and letting go, finding freedom in releasing the burdens that hinder our joy and peace.

The call to forgive is not an easy one, for it requires us to confront our pain, extend grace, and surrender our desire for justice. Yet, when we examine God's Word, we see that forgiveness is at the core of His redemptive plan. Through Christ's sacrifice, we have received the gift of forgiveness, and we are called to extend that same forgiveness to others.

Forgiveness does not excuse or condone the hurt inflicted upon us, nor does it negate the consequences of the actions committed. Instead, it is a deliberate choice to release the power that pain and bitterness hold over our lives. It is a conscious decision to let go of the chains that bind us, allowing God to heal and restore our wounded hearts.

Sisters, when we choose to forgive, we are not only granting freedom to those who have wronged us, but we are also liberating ourselves. Unforgiveness keeps us trapped in a cycle of resentment, anger, and negativity. But through forgiveness, we open the door for healing, restoration, and a renewed sense of purpose.

Letting go is not a one-time event but a continuous process. It begins with acknowledging our pain and bringing it before our Heavenly Father, who understands our hurt and offers comfort and solace. We can be vulnerable before Him, pouring out our emotions and seeking His guidance in the journey of forgiveness.

We must also remember that forgiveness is not dependent on the actions or attitudes of the other person. It is an act of obedience to God's command and a reflection of His character within us. In forgiving, we choose to break the cycle of hurt and vengeance, allowing God to be the ultimate judge and source of justice.

As we extend forgiveness, we are called to bear with one another and to foster an atmosphere of grace and compassion. This includes forgiving ourselves for past mistakes and shortcomings. God's forgiveness knows no bounds, and He invites us to receive His grace, embracing the opportunity for growth and transformation.

Sisters, forgiving does not mean forgetting or necessarily restoring a broken relationship. It means releasing the hold that the offense has on our hearts and entrusting the outcome to God. It means embracing the freedom to move forward, unencumbered by the weight of the past.

In the process of forgiveness, we may experience moments of struggle, doubt, or relapse. But in those moments, let us turn to God, who is faithful to help us persevere. His Spirit within us provides the strength and grace needed to forgive, even in the face of great pain.

Today, let us take a step towards forgiveness and letting go. May we surrender our hurts and grievances to our Heavenly Father, trusting in His power to heal and restore. Through forgiveness, may we find freedom, peace, and a renewed sense of purpose in serving others and reflecting the love of our forgiving Savior.

Prayer:

Gracious Father,

We come before You with hearts burdened by pain and hurt. We acknowledge the struggles we face in forgiving those who have wronged us. Today, we choose to walk the path of forgiveness, surrendering our pain to Your loving care. Help us dear Lord to grow closer to you in this hour and to seek your face more.

Prayer:

Heavenly Father,

We bow before You, recognizing Your great mercy and grace. Today, we bring before You the women who carry the heavy burdens of unforgiveness and the struggle to let go. We ask for Your divine intervention, Your healing touch, and Your guidance as we embark on a journey of forgiveness and release.

Lord, we acknowledge the pain and hurt that have wounded our hearts. We confess that holding onto resentment and bitterness only deepens our wounds, keeping us captive to the past. Today, we choose to release those who have caused us harm, surrendering our right to hold onto the offenses committed against us.

In the midst of our pain, help us to see the example of Your Son, Jesus Christ, who willingly forgave those who crucified Him. Teach us to extend the same forgiveness to others, for You have forgiven us of our own sins. Grant us the strength and humility to let go, knowing that forgiveness is a reflection of Your character and love within us.

Lord, we lift up those who have hurt us, whether intentionally or unknowingly. We release them from the debts they owe us and place them into Your hands. Help us to see them through Your eyes of compassion and grant us the grace to pray for their well-being and transformation.

As we forgive, we also ask for the courage to forgive ourselves. Too often, we carry the weight of guilt and shame, unable to let go of our own mistakes and shortcomings. Remind us that Your grace is greater than our failures and that Your forgiveness knows no limits. Enable us to embrace the freedom that comes from accepting Your forgiveness and extending it to ourselves.

Lord, we understand that forgiveness does not mean forgetting or necessarily reconciling with those who have hurt us. We entrust the healing and restoration of relationships to Your sovereign hands, trusting that You will work according to Your perfect will. Give us wisdom to set healthy boundaries and to walk in discernment as we navigate these complexities.

In moments of weakness or doubt, strengthen us by Your Holy Spirit. Fill us with Your peace that surpasses all understanding and guard our hearts from the temptation to dwell on the past. Help us to focus on the present, trusting that You are making all things new.

Thank You, Lord, for the freedom that comes through forgiveness and letting go. May we experience the joy and peace that arise from releasing the burdens that have weighed us down. May our lives reflect Your love and grace as we extend forgiveness to others, just as You have forgiven us.

In the name of Jesus, the ultimate Forgiver, we pray. Amen.

Day 9

Honoring Self-Care and Restoration

Scripture:

"Do you not know that your bodies are temples of the Holy Spirit, who is in you, whom you have received from God? You are not your own; you were bought at a price. Therefore, honor God with your bodies." - 1 Corinthians 6:19-20

Dear Sisters,

In the busyness of life, it is all too easy to neglect our own well-being—physically, emotionally, and spiritually. We pour ourselves into caring for others, meeting deadlines, and fulfilling responsibilities, often leaving little time and energy for ourselves. But today, let us explore the vital importance of self-care and devotion, recognizing that nurturing our souls is an act of worship and a reflection of God's love for us.

Jesus, our greatest example, modeled the significance of self-care and devotion. Despite the demands placed upon Him, He intentionally withdrew to spend time alone with His Heavenly Father. In these moments of solitude, He found refreshment, guidance, and renewed strength to continue His ministry.

Sisters, we are called to follow in the footsteps of our Savior. Just as Jesus prioritized time for prayer and solitude, we too must create space in our lives for self-care and devotion. This intentional act of nurturing our souls enables us to align ourselves with God's will, receive His guidance, and experience His peace in the midst of life's challenges.

Self-care is not selfish; it is an act of stewardship. It involves intentionally tending to our physical, emotional, and spiritual needs, recognizing that we cannot pour from an empty cup. It means setting boundaries, saying no when necessary, and giving ourselves permission to rest and recharge.

Physical self-care encompasses nourishing our bodies through healthy eating, regular exercise, and adequate rest. It involves listening to our bodies, caring for any ailments or discomfort, and prioritizing activities that bring us joy and vitality. Remember, dear sisters, that our bodies are temples of the Holy Spirit (1 Corinthians 6:19), and honoring them is an act of worship.

Emotional self-care involves tending to our hearts and minds. It means being mindful of our emotions, acknowledging them without judgment, and seeking healthy outlets for processing and expressing them. It includes engaging in activities that bring us joy, practicing self-compassion, and cultivating healthy relationships that nurture our emotional well-being.

Spiritual self-care is the foundation of our devotion to God. It involves carving out time for prayer, studying His Word, and engaging in spiritual practices that deepen our relationship with Him. It means seeking moments of solitude and stillness, allowing ourselves to be filled with His presence, and aligning our hearts with His purposes.

As we prioritize self-care and devotion, we must remember that our ultimate goal is not self-indulgence or self-centeredness. Rather, it is to nurture our souls so that we may serve others from a place of wholeness, love, and abundance. It is an act of surrender, recognizing that our well-being is intricately connected to our ability to fulfill the purposes God has placed before us.

Dear sisters, let us commit to the intentional practice of self-care and devotion. May we create sacred spaces in our lives, where we can encounter God's presence, find restoration, and be filled with His love. As we care for ourselves, may our lives radiate His grace, compassion, and joy, drawing others into the transformative power of His love.

Prayer:

Gracious Father,

We come before You with hearts in need of restoration and renewal. Thank You for reminding us of the importance of self-care and devotion. Help us to prioritize these practices in our lives, understanding that they are not selfish but essential for our well-being.

In the busyness of life, grant us the wisdom to set healthy boundaries and to say no when necessary. Fill us with the courage to prioritize our physical

Prayer:

We humbly come before Your throne, recognizing Your deep love and care for us as Your daughters. Today, we lift up the women in need of self-care and restoration. We acknowledge that we often neglect our own well-being, leaving us weary and in need of Your healing touch.

Lord, we surrender our burdens and responsibilities to You. We confess that we have allowed the demands of life to consume us, neglecting our physical, emotional, and spiritual needs. Today, we ask for Your forgiveness and guidance as we embark on a journey of self-care and restoration.

Father, we pray for physical strength and vitality. Grant us wisdom to nourish our bodies with wholesome food, exercise, and rest. Help us to listen to the signals of our bodies and to care for ourselves as vessels of Your Spirit. We invite You to heal any physical ailments or weariness, granting us the energy and stamina to fulfill our callings.

Emotionally, we bring before You the burdens, anxieties, and wounds that we carry. Heal our hearts, O Lord, from past hurts and disappointments. Grant us the courage to face our emotions, to process them in healthy ways, and to seek support and guidance when needed. Fill us with Your peace that surpasses all understanding, anchoring our souls in Your love.

Spiritually, we yearn for restoration and renewal. Draw us closer to Your heart, O God, as we carve out sacred moments for prayer, meditation, and study of Your Word. Help us to create space in our lives for solitude and silence, that we may hear Your gentle whisper and experience Your presence. Restore our souls, that we may be filled afresh with Your Spirit.

Lord, we pray for restoration in our relationships. Heal any broken-ness, strife, or bitterness that may exist. Teach us to extend forgiveness and grace, both to ourselves and to others. Guide us in cultivating healthy connections and setting boundaries that honor Your plans for our lives. May our relationships be a source of support, encourage-ment, and mutual growth.

In the midst of our self-care and restoration, remind us that our ul-timate reliance is on You. You are our Great Restorer, the One who mends our brokenness and makes all things new. We surrender our-selves to Your loving care, trusting that as we draw near to You, You will draw near to us.

Father, thank You for Your boundless love and grace. As we prioritize self-care and restoration, may we be transformed by Your Spirit. May our lives reflect Your peace, joy, and wholeness, drawing others into the embrace of Your love.

In the name of Jesus, our Redeemer and Healer, we pray. Amen.

Day 10

Embracing Divine Purpose and Abundance

Scripture:

"For I know the plans I have for you," declares the LORD, "plans to prosper you and not to harm you, plans to give you hope and a future." - Jeremiah 29:11

Scripture:

"For we are God's handiwork, created in Christ Jesus to do good works, which God prepared in advance for us to do." - Ephesians 2:10 (NIV)

Devotional:

Dear Sisters,

In the depths of our hearts, we long for purpose and meaning in our lives. We desire to make a difference, to contribute to something greater than ourselves. Today, let us embark on a journey of discovering and embracing our divine purpose, understanding that each one of us has been uniquely created by God for a specific calling.

As women, we may often find ourselves wearing various hats and fulfilling multiple roles—mothers, wives, daughters, friends, professionals, and more. In the midst of our diverse responsibilities, it is easy to lose sight of our unique purpose. But remember, dear sisters, that God has intricately designed each one of us with a specific plan in mind.

Our purpose begins with recognizing that we are God's handiwork, fearfully and wonderfully made in His image. We are not accidents or mistakes; we are intentional creations with unique gifts, talents, and passions. Our purpose is not defined by societal expectations or comparisons to others but by the One who lovingly fashioned us.

To discover our purpose, we must first seek God's guidance through prayer and reflection. As we draw near to Him, He reveals His plans for our lives. It may not come in one grand revelation but through a series of small steps, nudges, and confirmations. Pay attention to the desires and passions that stir within your heart, for they may be indications of the calling God has placed on your life.

Our purpose is not solely about personal fulfillment; it is about participating in God's redemptive work in the world. It is about serving others, sharing His love, and making a positive impact in our spheres of influence. Whether it be in our families, workplaces, communities, or beyond, God invites us to use our unique gifts and talents to bring hope, healing, and transformation.

In the pursuit of purpose, we must also embrace a spirit of surrender. Our plans and desires may not always align with God's greater purposes, but His ways are higher and His plans are perfect. Trust in His sovereignty and wisdom, knowing that He will guide us along the path He has prepared for us.

Sisters, let us not be discouraged by setbacks or moments of uncertainty. Instead, let us draw strength from knowing that our purpose is not defined by our circumstances or achievements, but by our faithfulness in obediently following God's lead. Even in the mundane tasks and ordinary moments of life, we can fulfill our purpose by seeking to reflect God's love and character to those around us.

Lastly, our purpose is not a destination but a lifelong journey. It evolves and unfolds as we grow in our relationship with God and experience His transforming work within us. Be open to His redirection and refinement, knowing that He is constantly shaping us into vessels that can be used for His glory.

Prayer:

Dear Heavenly Father,

Thank You for creating us with a unique purpose. As women, we long to fulfill the calling You have placed upon our lives. We surrender our plans and desires to You, trusting that Your purposes for us are greater than we can comprehend.

Guide us, Lord, as we seek to discover our divine purpose. Open our eyes to see the gifts, talents, and passions You have instilled within us. Help us to discern Your voice amidst the noise of the world and to trust Your leading.

As we embark on this journey, grant us the courage to step out in faith. Fill us with Your wisdom and strength, that we may make a positive impact in the

lives of those around us. Help us to serve others selflessly, reflecting Your love and grace in all that we do.

Lord, in moments of doubt or confusion, remind us of Your unwavering faithfulness. Give us the perseverance to press on, knowing that You are with us every step of the way. May our lives bring glory to Your name as we walk in the fullness of our purpose.

In Jesus' name, we pray. Amen.

Day 11

Rise and Shine forth for Jesus

Scripture:

"I can do all things through Christ who strengthens me." - Philippians 4:13 (NKJV)

Devotional:

Dear Sisters,

In a world filled with challenges and uncertainties, it is time for us, as women of faith, to rise forth in Jesus. We are called to step into the fullness of our identity and embrace the unique calling He has placed upon our lives. Through Him, we have the strength, courage, and power to overcome any obstacle and fulfill our purpose.

Jesus came to this earth and shattered societal norms, elevating the status of women and empowering them to be His followers and disciples. He saw the value and worth in each woman He encountered, inviting them to experience His love, grace, and redemption. Today, He extends the same invitation to us.

Sisters, it is time to rise forth in Jesus, recognizing that our worth is not determined by the world's standards, but by the truth of God's Word. We are fearfully and wonderfully made, created in His image, and endowed with unique gifts and talents. We are daughters of the Most High God, cherished and loved beyond measure.

To rise forth in Jesus means to fully embrace our identity as His beloved children. It means rejecting the lies of inadequacy, comparison, and self-doubt. Instead, we cling to the truth that we are chosen, called, and equipped by Him. Our confidence is not in our own abilities but in the power of Christ working within us.

As we rise forth in Jesus, we must also seek His guidance and direction. He has a specific calling and purpose for each one of us. It may look different for each woman, but it is equally significant in His kingdom. Whether it be in our homes, workplaces, communities, or beyond, He invites us to use our gifts and talents to make a difference for His glory.

Rising forth in Jesus requires courage and boldness. We may face opposition, doubt, and discouragement along the way. But remember, dear sisters, that the same power that raised Jesus from the grave resides within us. We are not alone. The Holy Spirit empowers us, equips us, and strengthens us for the tasks set before us.

Let us not be bound by the limitations that others may try to impose upon us. Instead, let us rise forth in Jesus, embracing the freedom and authority that comes from being His followers. May our lives be a testament to His transformative power, demonstrating His love, grace, and compassion to a world in need.

Sisters, as we rise forth in Jesus, let us also support and encourage one another. Together, we are a powerful force for His kingdom. Let us celebrate the successes, lift each other up in prayer, and walk alongside one another as we fulfill our individual callings.

Prayer:

Dear Heavenly Father,

Thank You for calling us to rise forth in Jesus. Today, we embrace our identity as Your beloved daughters, fearfully and wonderfully made. Help us to reject the lies of inadequacy and to walk confidently in the truth of Your Word.

Lord, we surrender our lives to Your guidance and direction. Show us the specific calling and purpose You have for each one of us. Grant us the courage and boldness to step out in faith, knowing that You are with us every step of the way.

As we rise forth in Jesus, fill us with Your Holy Spirit. Empower us, equip us, and strengthen us to overcome any obstacle that stands in our path. May our lives bring glory to Your name as we reflect Your love, grace, and power. In Jesus' name, we pray. Amen.

Day 12

Arise with God's Favor

Scripture:

"For you bless the righteous, O Lord; you cover him with favor as with a shield."
- Psalm 5:12 (ESV)

Devotional:

Dear Sisters,

In the journey of faith, we are invited to arise in the favor of God. His favor is not something we can earn or achieve through our own efforts, but rather a lavish gift bestowed upon us by His grace. Today, let us explore the incredible blessings that come with walking in the favor of our Heavenly Father.

God's favor is an expression of His deep love and kindness toward His children. It is His divine smile upon us, showering us with His unmerited blessings and goodness. When we walk in His favor, doors open, obstacles are overcome, and His provision abounds in every area of our lives.

Arising in the favor of God begins with an understanding of our righteousness in Christ. Through Jesus' sacrifice on the cross, we have been made righteous, justified before God, and reconciled to Him. As we embrace this truth, we can approach God with boldness, knowing that His favor rests upon us.

Walking in God's favor requires surrendering our own agendas and aligning our hearts with His will. It means seeking His guidance and direction in every decision we make. As we prioritize His kingdom and seek His righteousness, He pours out His favor upon us, leading us to paths of blessing and fulfillment.

In the favor of God, we find supernatural provision and abundance. It is not limited to material blessings alone, but encompasses His provision of wisdom, strength, and grace in every circumstance. When we acknowledge His favor, we can trust that He will meet our needs according to His glorious riches.

As women of faith, we are called to arise in the favor of God, not only for our own benefit but also for the sake of others. When we walk in His favor, we become vessels of His love, grace, and power. We can be instruments of transformation and blessing in our families, workplaces, communities, and beyond.

However, let us remember that God's favor does not exempt us from challenges or hardships. We may still face trials and difficulties along the way. But even in the midst of these, we can trust that His favor surrounds us like a shield, protecting us and empowering us to overcome.

Arising in the favor of God also means extending His favor to others. Just as we have received His unmerited blessings, we are called to extend grace, love, and kindness to those around us. We have the privilege of being conduits of His favor, bringing hope and encouragement to those who need it.

Prayer:

Gracious Heavenly Father,

Thank You for Your abundant favor that rests upon us. We are humbled by Your unmerited blessings and the lavish love You pour out upon us. Today, we arise in Your favor, embracing the incredible privilege of walking in Your grace.

Lord, help us to understand our righteousness in Christ and to approach You with boldness. Guide us in surrendering our lives to Your will and seeking Your kingdom above all else. May we experience the fullness of Your favor in every area of our lives.

In moments of challenge and adversity, remind us that Your favor surrounds us like a shield. Strengthen us and empower us to overcome, knowing that Your favor goes before us. Use us as vessels of Your love and grace, that we may bring hope and transformation to those around us.

Thank You, Lord, for the incredible privilege of arising in Your favor. May our lives bring glory to Your name as we walk in the fullness of Your blessings.

In Jesus' name, we pray.

Amen.

Prayer:

Heavenly Father,

We come before Your throne with grateful hearts, recognizing Your unfailing love and grace toward us as Your daughters. Today, we humbly seek Your favor, knowing that in Your favor, we find blessings, guidance, and supernatural provision.

Lord, we acknowledge that Your favor is not something we can earn or achieve through our own efforts. It is a precious gift, given to us by Your grace and mercy. We thank You for extending Your favor upon our lives and for the incredible blessings that flow from it.

In Your favor, we find wisdom and discernment. We ask for Your guidance and direction in every aspect of our lives. Lead us on the path of righteousness, aligning our hearts with Your will. Help us to make decisions that honor You and bring glory to Your name.

Father, in Your favor, we find provision and abundance. You are the source of all good things, and we trust in Your provision for our needs. Open the windows of heaven and pour out Your blessings upon us, both spiritually and materially. Fill our lives with Your abundance, that we may overflow with generosity and bless others.

Lord, in Your favor, we find protection and strength. Surround us with Your presence and cover us with Your mighty shield. Guard us from the schemes of the enemy and shield us from harm. Empower us with

Your strength to overcome any obstacles or challenges that come our way.

Father, we pray for favor in our relationships and endeavors. Open doors of opportunity for us, granting us favor with others. May our interactions be marked by kindness, respect, and understanding. Help us to be a positive influence and a shining light in every sphere of our lives.

Above all, Lord, may Your favor rest upon us so that we may be vessels of Your love and grace. Use us to bring hope, encouragement, and healing to those around us. May our lives reflect Your goodness and draw others into a relationship with You.

We surrender ourselves to Your will, knowing that Your favor is greater than any earthly recognition or success. May Your favor lead us to a deeper intimacy with You and a greater understanding of Your purposes for our lives.

We thank You, Lord, for Your unending favor and for the privilege of being Your beloved daughters. May Your favor continue to rest upon us, transforming our lives and enabling us to fulfill our calling. In Jesus' name, we pray. Amen.

Day 13

You were born for this moment

Scripture:

"And who knows but that you have come to your royal position for such a time as this?" - Esther 4:14b (NIV)

Devotional:

Dear Sisters,

In every generation, God raises up men and women with a specific purpose and calling. You, dear sister, have been born for such a time as this. Just like the brave Queen Esther, who stepped forward in a critical moment, you are uniquely positioned to make a significant impact in your sphere of influence.

God has placed you here and now, with your unique gifts, talents, and experiences, for a divine purpose. He has intricately woven together every detail of your life to prepare you for this moment in history. You are not here by accident but by His deliberate design.

It is easy to underestimate our significance or doubt our abilities. But let me remind you, dear sister, that you are fearfully and wonderfully made. God has equipped you with everything you need to fulfill your purpose. He has deposited within you the gifts, strengths, and passions that align with His plans for your life.

You may face challenges and uncertainties along the way, but God's presence and guidance will never leave you. Just as He was with Esther, He is with you. He will go before you, making a way where there seems to be no way. Trust in His faithfulness and lean on His wisdom as you navigate the path set before you.

Embracing your purpose requires boldness and courage. Like Esther, you may need to step out of your comfort zone, speak up for justice, and take risks. But remember that the same God who called you is the one who empowers and strengthens you. With Him by your side, you can face any obstacle with confidence.

In times of uncertainty, seek God's face and listen to His voice. Spend time in prayer and study His Word, for it is through His Word that He imparts wisdom, direction, and revelation. Allow His Spirit to guide you, opening your eyes to the opportunities and possibilities that lie before you.

Remember, your purpose extends beyond your personal fulfillment. It is intertwined with God's redemptive plan for the world. As you live out your purpose, you become an instrument of His love, grace, and transformation. Your words, actions, and influence can bring hope and healing to those around you.

Dear sister, embrace the truth that you were born for such a time as this. Your life has a unique purpose and calling that only you can fulfill. Trust in God's guidance, rely on His strength, and step forward with boldness. As you do, you will witness the incredible ways in which He uses your life to impact others and bring glory to His name.

Prayer:

Heavenly Father,

Thank You for creating me with a purpose and calling. Help me to fully embrace the truth that I was born for such a time as this. Equip me with Your wisdom, courage, and strength to fulfill the divine assignment You have entrusted to me.

In moments of doubt or uncertainty, remind me of Your presence and faithfulness. Give me the boldness to step out in obedience, even when the path ahead seems unclear. I trust in Your guidance and provision, knowing that You are with me every step of the way.

Open my eyes to the opportunities and possibilities that lie before me.

Help me to discern Your voice and to align my life with Your will. Use me as an instrument of Your love, grace, and transformation in the world.

May my life bring glory to Your name, as I fulfill the purpose for which You created me. In all things, may Your kingdom come and Your will be done.

In Jesus' name

Prayer:

Gracious Father,

We come before You with hearts full of gratitude and awe, recognizing Your sovereign plan and purpose for each of our lives. We thank You for designing us, as women, to be born for such a time as this. We acknowledge that You have positioned us in this generation with intention and divine appointments.

Lord, we surrender ourselves to Your purposes and plans. We trust that You have equipped us with unique gifts, talents, and passions to make a difference in the world around us. Help us to embrace our calling and step boldly into the roles You have prepared for us.

In moments of doubt or insecurity, remind us of Your faithfulness throughout history. You have used ordinary men and women to accomplish extraordinary things for Your kingdom. Just as You empowered Esther, Deborah, Ruth, and countless others, we trust that You will empower us to fulfill our purpose in this time.

Father, grant us wisdom and discernment to navigate the complexities of our world. Guide our steps and help us to make choices that align with Your will. Open our eyes to the needs and opportunities around us, that we may be agents of transformation and vessels of Your love.

We pray for strength and courage to face the challenges that come with our calling. When fear or discouragement arise, remind us of Your presence and the promises in Your Word. Fill us with Your Spirit, that we may walk in boldness, trusting in Your unfailing grace and power.

Lord, we intercede for women everywhere who are still discovering their purpose or struggling to embrace it. May they be filled with a deep sense of purpose and identity in You. Illuminate their path and give them the confidence to step forward and make an impact in their spheres of influence.

Father, we ask for unity among women, transcending differences and embracing the strength of our diversity. Help us to celebrate and support one another, lifting each other up in prayer and encouragement. May we be a sisterhood that stands together, empowering and inspiring one another to fulfill our God-given destinies.

We thank You, Lord, for the privilege of being born for such a time as this. May Your Holy Spirit continue to guide us, empower us, and lead us into the purposes You have prepared for us. Use our lives to bring glory to Your name and to advance Your kingdom in every sphere of society.

In Jesus' mighty name, we pray.

Amen.

Day 14

Rise up as finishers

Scripture:

"I have fought the good fight, I have finished the race, I have kept the faith." - 2 Timothy 4:7 (NIV)

Devotional:

Dear Sisters,

In the journey of faith, we are called not only to start well but also to finish strong. As women, we have the incredible capacity to rise up as finishers, embracing perseverance and faithfulness in every area of our lives. Today, let us explore what it means to be women who complete what we have started and finish the race set before us.

In a world filled with distractions, challenges, and obstacles, it can be tempting to give up or lose sight of our goals and aspirations. However, we are called to press on, to rise above adversity, and to remain steadfast until the end. Like athletes running a race, we are encouraged to keep our eyes fixed on the ultimate prize—our eternal reward in Christ.

To rise up as finishers, we must first cultivate a spirit of perseverance. This means embracing a mindset that acknowledges setbacks and difficulties as opportunities for growth and transformation. Instead of being discouraged by obstacles, we can view them as stepping stones toward our ultimate goal. Let us lean on God's strength and rely on His grace to carry us through the challenges we face.

In our pursuit of finishing well, it is crucial to remember that our source of strength and endurance comes from the Lord. We cannot rely solely on our own abilities or willpower. Instead, we can draw upon His power and rely on the Holy Spirit's guidance to empower us to persevere. As we abide in Him and trust in His faithfulness, He equips us to press on and finish strong.

As women, we often juggle multiple responsibilities and wear numerous hats. In the midst of our many tasks and commitments, it is vital to prioritize what truly matters. We must discern God's will for our lives and align our actions with His purposes. By focusing on what He has called us to do, we can channel our energy and efforts into areas of significance, allowing us to finish what we have started.

Rising up as finishers also requires a commitment to faithfulness. It means being consistent, diligent, and faithful in the small things. Our faithfulness in the seemingly insignificant tasks prepares us for greater opportunities and positions of influence. Let us remember that faithfulness is not just about completing tasks, but also about being faithful stewards of the gifts, talents, and relationships entrusted to us.

In the process of finishing well, we must guard against distractions and complacency. The enemy seeks to divert our attention and hinder our progress. We must remain vigilant and focused, constantly seeking the Lord's guidance and discernment. With His help, we can navigate through the distractions and stay on course until we reach the finish line.

Dear sisters, as we rise up as finishers.

Prayer:

Gracious Father,

We come before You, our source of strength and grace, seeking Your guidance and empowerment to finish strong in every area of our lives. We acknowledge that the journey may be challenging, but we know that with Your presence and assistance, we can overcome every obstacle and persevere until the end.

Lord, we surrender our fears, doubts, and insecurities to You. Fill our hearts with unwavering faith and confidence in Your promises. Help us to fix our eyes on Jesus, who endured the cross for the joy set before Him. May His example inspire us to press on, knowing that our efforts are not in vain.

Father, grant us the discipline and perseverance to stay committed to the tasks and assignments You have entrusted to us. When weariness sets in, remind us of Your abundant grace and strength available to us. Help us to rely on You, drawing from Your wellspring of endurance and determination.

We pray for clarity and wisdom to prioritize our time and efforts according to Your will. Guide us in discerning what is truly important and aligning our pursuits with Your purposes. Grant us the courage to let go of distractions and unnecessary burdens that hinder our progress.

Lord, we ask for Your divine favor to rest upon us as we journey toward the finish line. Open doors of opportunity, provide divine connections, and supply the resources we need to accomplish Your plans for our lives. Let Your favor go before us, making a way where there seems to be no way.

Help us to embrace the lessons and growth that come with perseverance. Teach us to learn from setbacks, failures, and disappointments, trusting that You can turn them into stepping stones toward greater victories. Strengthen our resilience, that we may rise above challenges with grace and determination.

Father, as we strive to finish strong, remind us that our ultimate purpose is to bring glory to Your name. May our efforts and accomplishments point others to Your goodness and faithfulness. Use us as instruments of Your love, grace, and hope in a world that desperately needs You.

In all things, may Your will be done. Give us hearts that are surrendered to Your plans and purposes. Grant us the endurance and perseverance to finish strong, knowing that our reward is not merely in earthly accolades but in the eternal blessings You have prepared for us.

We pray this in the mighty name of Jesus, who is our ultimate example of finishing strong. Amen.

Final Thoughts

Rise Up Women of God prayer journal is a daily prayer journal that takes you on a transformative journey through ten empowering chapters. Each chapter focuses on a specific theme, accompanied by carefully selected scriptures to inspire and guide your prayerful reflections. As you engage with the prompts, scriptural passages, and your own heartfelt prayers, Rise Up Women of God prayer journal invites you to deepen your spiritual connection, experience divine love, find inner strength, and embrace the abundant life that awaits you. May this journal be a source of encouragement, healing, and divine revelation as you cultivate a vibrant and radiant spirit.

About The Author

Dr. Monique Rodgers is an ordained prophet, visionary, intercessor, international best-selling author, CEO, motivational speaker, entrepreneur, educator, and literary genius. Dr. Rodgers excels today as a notable writing coach, founder, and serial entrepreneur.

Throughout the course of her career, she has written such prolific works such as, Hello! My name is Millennial, Picking up the Pieces, The Majestical Land of Twinville, Falling in Love with Jesus, Accelerate, Overcoming Writer's Block, Just Breathe, and Called to Intercede Volumes 1-4. She has also been included as a co-author in collaborations such as, Jumpstart Your Mind, Speak Up We Deserve to Be Heard, Finding Joy in the Journey Volume 2, and Let the Kingdompreneurs Speak. Due to her outstanding breadth of experience, Dr. Rodgers has been featured on Rachel Speaks radio program, The Love Walk Podcast, The Glory Network, God's Glory Radio Show, The Miracle Zone, The Healing Zone. She also graced several platforms worldwide. She served as a TV host for WATCTV. She has been featured in Heart and Soul Magazine, My Story the Magazine, Kish Magazine's Top 20 National Authors of 2021. Marquis Who's Who in America

2021-2022. She also assisted in various volunteer work including an executive team member for Lady Deliverer's Arise, Aniyah Space and she also a board member for I am my sister organization. She is also a certified master business coach, certified vegan life coach, and health advocate. She has served on various leadership positions in business and in ministry. She is currently a prayer hub leader for the city of Raleigh under the tutelage of Apostle Jennifer LeClaire. She is also a team member of CBK where she serves in ministry for Sofia Ruffin. As an expert in her field Dr. Rodgers earned her undergraduate degree through Oral Roberts University as well as a Master of Science degree and a doctorate in global leadership through Colorado Technical University. She has also studied at the Black Business School online as well as Harvard University Business Online. Looking towards the future, Dr. Rodgers intends to expand upon her expertise and continue serving through ministry for God. She aspires to help over one hundred authors to complete and publish their books and help intercessors to draw closer to God.

To stay connected with Dr. Monique Rodgers

Contact information:

www.getwriteoncoaching.com

Facebook: www.facebook.com/moniquerodgers2

Instagram: @drroyalty7

Twitter: @DrMonique7

LinkedIn: Dr. Monique Rodgers

YouTube: Dr. Monique Rodgers

Clubhouse: @DrMonique7

Email: calledtointerecede@gmail.com